For Jim and Pamela Morton

Translations of works by the same author :

This day belongs to God, Faith Press, London.

Unity man's tomorrow, Faith Press, London ;
Herder and Herder, New York.

The power of the provisional, Hodder and
Stoughton, London.

Unanimity in pluralism, Franciscan Herald
Press, Chicago.

Violent for peace, Darton, Longman & Todd,
London.

The Rule of Taizé, Les Presses de Taizé.

Festival

BROTHER ROGER
Prior of Taizé

TRANSLATED BY BRETHREN
OF THE TAIZÉ COMMUNITY

LONDON
SPCK

First published in French 1971
with the title *Ta fête soit sans fin*
by Les Presses de Taizé.

© The Publishers 1971

First published in English 1973
by Les Presses de Taizé.

Reissued 1974
by SPCK
Holy Trinity Church
Marylebone Road
London NW1 4DU

© Les Presses de Taizé 1973

Printed by offset in Great Britain by
The Camelot Press Ltd, Southampton

SBN 281 02792 7

CONTENTS

In these pages I try to be open, setting illusions aside.

The knowledge of my poverty allows me to be myself.

By his poverty man loves, creates, struggles, marvels : but he pays a high price for his freedom.

IF FESTIVITY WERE TO VANISH...

If festivity were to vanish from men's lives...

If we were going to awake, one fine morning, in a society that was well organised, functional and contented — but devoid of any spontaneity...

If christians' prayer were becoming a sheer intellectual exercise, so secularised as to have lost all sense of mystery and poetry, with no place for the body to pray, no room for intuitions or for the affections...

If the overburdened conscience of christians caused them to say no to a happiness offered them by the One who, seven times over, proclaimed 'happy' on the Mount of the Beatitudes...

If those living in the northern hemisphere, worn out by activities, were to lose the source of the spirit of festival — when that festival is still so alive in the hearts of the peoples of the southern continents...

If festivity faded away from the body of Christ, the Church, where on the earth could there still be found a single reality of communion for the whole of mankind ?

It is thirst for communion that I sense in the young people here on the hill. For them, as for every generation, it is strong to the point of anguish :

— Communion with man in his struggles and aspirations, although these are years that are witnessing a crisis of confidence in mankind.

10

— Communion with Christ. For many, simply to hold oneself before God is so important — whether or not they can achieve some dialogue within this confrontation.

If the festival within me faded out, would I still have the energy to keep searching, ever anew, for communion with the rising generations ?

I know from experience how hard the first contact with them can be. To begin with they are on their guard in the presence of men bearing the charge of authority ; their first question is often abrupt. They need to test the temperature of the man who is here before them with his years, his past, his white alb with the cross of Christ lying on it. And there can be no running away from this ; what counts is to listen, so that trust can break through. There comes a change in the way

11

of looking. And to find some kind of reply, I search deep within myself for some word, some image. And may be it is I who am most surprised of all by the words I utter.

Week after week, at the end of the common prayer, I attempt to answer questions prepared by some of the young people. Often I am forced to say : all I can do is give you the beginnings of an answer — expressing aloud what is really a kind of dialogue with myself. It is up to you to pursue it within yourselves.

How to make oneself understood in the presence of so many different mentalities and nationalities ? There are days when I am not sure how to tread : some people come to Taizé in a last attempt to find something in the Church. Are my words going to drive them away for good, and without any hope ? But if festivity were to vanish . . .

Dialogue

FESTIVAL IN STRUGGLE

Brother Roger, could you say something more about what you mean when you speak of 'festival'? For us, festival first of all means being free from constraint; freedom, spontaneity : but all through our daily life we find limits being imposed on us.

Yes, spontaneity and freedom are to do with festival.

Festival is a small field that each of us has to cultivate within himself, a tiny playground for exercising freedom and spontaneity. True, there is a limit to this field : I cannot do violence to another's conscience, or make him my prisoner. From a little corner of spontaneity festival sings out in man, just as long as he does not violate some other person's freedom, but consents to his creativity.

In every man lies a zone of solitude that no human intimacy can fill : and there God encounters us. There, in that depth, is set the intimate festival of the risen Christ.

So henceforth, in the hollow of our being, we discover the risen Christ : he is our festival.

But how can we live and talk about festivity when we know all the things that keep men's lives from being festive : wars, suffering, injustice in all its forms ?

Knowing about present-day catastrophes, wars, ill-treated racial minorities, is unbearable. A man advancing in age is perhaps even more touched by such happenings, after a long christian life has rendered him increasingly sensitive. The intolerable thing is human distress, man for us being sacred. How could we bear to remain inactive where man is victim of man ?

But is our thirst for greater justice going to make us reject the intimate festival offered to every christian ? Then all that would remain would be for us to bow beneath the burden of our despair and offer our sadness to all mankind.

Could a life of festival really prevent someone from throwing himself into the struggle for justice ? Just the reverse. This festival is in no sense a moment's euphoria. It is brought into being by Christ in men and women who are completely clear about the situation the world is in, and are able to be open to the gravest events. But these men and women know that they are inhabited by the same need

17

to dominate and oppress as lies at the source of war and injustice. They know that the fight begins within themselves, if they are not to be, unawares, among the number of the oppressors.

Then even struggling becomes festival : the festivity of a struggle for Christ to be our essential love ; and the festivity of every struggle for those who are downtrodden.

Festival is bound up with the preparation of the Council of Youth. Can you tell us something about what brought you to announce this world-wide Council of Youth in 1970 ?

The idea of a Council of Youth was first born out of a failure : namely, the impasse in which the ecumenical vocation found itself, with so many people brutally rejecting the Church. Failure can become a driving force that enables us to overcome an obstacle.

18

After years of good ecumenical work — which brought results — are we not coming to a standstill ?

It is now several years since young people first began to tell me that the different christian confessions, whilst professing ecumenism, have settled down into a process of parallelism. We have moved away from mutual indifference between separated christians and have gone on to improve our relationships ; but none of that is leading to visible unity in the body of Jesus Christ. The various christian confessions continue their parallel existences and so fail to see why they should face the vital question of making unity visible. But without unity, how can a real welcome be offered ?

Seeing this, I was wondering what we could do. 'Ecumenism has reached a ceiling, who will find a way of breaking through ?'

19

In February 1969 the idea first began to come alive. We were surprised to find that the young people who had come to Taizé for the Shrove Tuesday holidays represented forty-two different countries. I found myself thinking : surely what we are experiencing together is a kind of un-expected council of youth ?

Their questions during those days were hard, and they keep on recurring : 'What should we do once we return home to our different countries ?' And I found myself unable to give them any real answer.

I soon decided that we could not go on without some kind of reply. If we just keep on telling them 'go back and carry on from where you are', that becomes an excuse for not trying. In spite of our-selves, our lack of any answer and our refusal to undertake some action mean that we are pushing many of them into agnosticism.

So it became essential to find a means of staying together, provisionally, yet over a certain period of time, and of asking one another the same questions all over the world in the same way, and yet without in any sense creating a new movement. Taizé has never founded any movement, just as there will never be a 'Taizé theology' or a 'Taizé spirituality'. Taizé is simply the name of a monastic family.

Ecumenism means 'the whole inhabited earth', all the men who live on the earth. There is no search for christian unity that does not include a desire to go everywhere and to join one with another. For a few days we had been able, without any preparation, to search together with young people from forty-two countries. By taking time and preparing ourselves beforehand, we could go a long way with young people from every country.

Then during the summer of 1969 I was inclined to reject the idea of a Council of Youth, reckoning that it went beyond our possibilities, and thinking too that we lacked the courage for such an undertaking. We began to look in other directions.

All through the summer a young woman from Buenos Aires, Margarita Moyano, was here leading the meetings ; General Secretary for Latin-American Catholic Youth, her presence signified a reciprocity between Latin America and Europe. She made us attentive to an appeal often repeated by young Latin-Americans : how « to make clearer the face of a Church that is truly poor, missionary and paschal, separated from all temporal powers and daringly committed to the liberation of every man and of all men » (Medellin Conference, 1968) ? We tried to find concrete ways of replying.

In the winter, the idea of holding a Council of Youth came back and it was then examined thoroughly with the intercontinental team that met at Taizé a fortnight before Easter 1970.

It took just over a year, from February 1969 to Easter 1970 for an idea, rejected then readopted, to be announced. And the driving force behind the announcement was an impasse that was closing us in more and more and out of which we were trying to find an exit.

Journal — extracts

FEBRUARY — JUNE 1969

When I chose the village of Taizé in 1940, I was alone. The silence of the deserts strengthens the encounter with God. Man alone with himself is sensitive to a presence alive within him.

It is not man's nature to dwell in the desert. All his attention is necessary if he is to comprehend a silence that is completely in-dwelling.

For a long period our life was marked not by isolation but by an accepted solitude. Nonetheless, from the very start our life at Taizé has been interwoven by encounters with others. After twenty years of common life we were thrown, so to speak, into the public arena. It has taken seven years, from 1962 to 1969, to circumscribe what was happening to us.

Whilst welcoming large numbers, we have always found ways of establishing zones of peace on the hill. I suspect that such simple values — silence, and also the love for things, for domestic animals — strengthen a creative capacity in us.

And now, during these days, young people from forty-two countries are gathered here quite unexpectedly in the depth of winter. We are exploring together. Forty-two countries : we are experiencing a kind of little council of youth.

These young people often have a great degree of selflessness. It comes from Christ. They shun privileges for themselves, and equally they cannot stand any caste-mentality. With them, the Church will go far.

22 February

Television teams in the church — camera-men who have arrived without warning. What can one say ? Their employers have sent them from a thousand kilometers away, one group from Rome, another from Germany. They are mostly family men. It would be inhuman simply to send them away.

I stress the need for total discretion. With high-sensitivity film they can avoid using flood-lights. But I know that they cannot do the impossible.

So before the start of the common prayer I am once again obliged to take the microphone and to explain to those present : 'Today, during our prayers, cameras will be on us for a few minutes. Some of us, because we take prayer so seriously, will find this invasion hard to accept. There are others, just as serious, who are glad of the possibility of communicating with great multitudes.'

23 February

A long talk with R. This brother questions me about the prayer that I improvise each day in the church at midday. He asks why, in it, I so often allude to darkness, to inner poverty, to night. Because I do not base my life on illusions. I know the combat being fought within the body of Christ, the Church. Certainly the Church will emerge from that combat : it does not die. Continually in a state of being born, it is created ever anew.

Of our obscurities, our own poverty, I will talk with God all the more readily since, at present, so many christians are conscious of their limits. And personally, I have no need to conceal my poverty. There, I contradict those who suppose that our vocation confers some privilege : like them, with them, I set out daily on the same road ; out of my night towards a light — or even, from doubt towards believing.

24 February

Not to confuse emotivity with sensitiveness. I refuse to be emotive (not the same as rare, deep emotions) : I have better use to make of my energies — they are already none too great. I refuse to be emotive, since my evolution — like that of our community, of the Church or of whole societies — does not at all depend on emotivity. Whereas sensitiveness remains vivid in many grave situations.

26 February

Bob Kennedy tells somewhere how difficult it was for those who met his brother, the president, to be themselves. Each visitor tended to enter into what he sensed of the president's line of thinking. One day, going with a friend to see his brother, he was astonished to hear his friend expressing the opposite of what he had determined to insist on. How can highly-placed statesmen be kept informed ?

And it is the same in the life of the Church. More than once I have been known to ask my brothers, before some conversation, to pray for me to remain myself and to keep my courage.

27 February

Afterwards, we shall be astonished to meet those who, not acquainted with Christ, have lived by him all unawares.

1 March

Several times in recent years, I have heard protestants (some of them pastors with personal positions of authority) repeat : 'Since the Vatican Council, the Catholic Church has replied to the questions posed by the Reformation, to the point that protestantism has lost its reasons for existing apart ; all its best aspirations are henceforth embodied in the Catholic Church. Is it now going to act in consequence, or invent new reasons to justify our separation ?'

And today arises the question : is not protest now in the act of taking over in the Catholic Church itself ? I should never have thought it, even a few years ago. The Reformation of the 16th century wished to protest against abuses, and to that, answer has been given. Today, within the Catholic Church, protesting does not necessarily have excess as its target — at times it becomes an end in itself. We are far from the point at which ecumenism began. A great storm has blown and at moments of calm we open our eyes wide, to see what has held firm.

2 March

Little Bruno baptised in the village church at Taizé. His parents are not involved in the life of the parish and so the priest had asked them to wait until later for the baptism. But when he saw their stupefaction and their real desire to understand, he finally agreed.

And what a festival ! Obvious astonishment on the part of the family. The grandfather is unable to recognise anything from previous occasions. He finds everything homely, accessible. I explain, 'It's because of the Council'. And a few days later he is heard to say, 'everything has properly changed, it's because of the consul'.

Back from the baptism, a brother tells me that a local man, the young father of a family, has just died. I remain silent in my room. This man, who spent all his holidays in his family home near Taizé, was almost unknown to me. His family held in conscience that no contact between us was possible for doctrinal reasons. Four days ago, on the morning marking the twenty-fifth anniversary of my first arrival in Taizé, I went to a mass celebrated by a priest of the same family — a true patriarch in the midst of his people. I had indicated that I should be there. The mass over, everyone left and I remained alone, waiting for the priest to emerge from the sacristy. Not seeing him come, I ventured to go to greet him. His welcome was, 'the Church is intransigent'. 'True', I replied, 'yet everywhere openings are being prepared'. And I attempted to explain all that we are involved in with catholics — those of Latin America for example.

4 March

This morning, a letter from the widow. Replying to a message I had sent, she writes : 'The assurance of the prayers of your community reached me at the very moment that the Lord called my husband to Himself . . . and since today I have the opportunity, I want to tell you how, although we never had the joy of talking with you, your thoughts have often been the source of our reflexion as a couple — perhaps particularly "Today belongs to God" which we frequently read and meditated over together.'

Already, beyond the divisions, there had been a contact. I am overwhelmed.

5 March

Among christians and atheists alike, too much vital energy is used up in constructing abstract, ideal forms of society ; at the end of it all, a lot of ideas but nothing is really achieved for mankind. Protest itself is now becoming another ideology, instead of being creative criticism.

I can see nothing more appalling than to live as an ideologist. Seek to free myself from ideologies — refuse the luxury of wasting the energies so much needed if the earth is to be made a place to live in.

6 March

Alternation, the provisional — two values I believe in profoundly ! But I know too that for some people they serve to disguise a basic dissatisfaction. As though change can have magical results. True, if a person ups roots, he finds a momentary sense of peace which distracts him to such an extent that he may believe he has really changed. But time goes by and the day comes when he finds himself once more confronted with himself. Basically, in spite of the uprooting, nothing had altered. And there he is, insatiable once more. Let's make a change — for me to stay where I am. Let's make a change, then I shall not have to pay what it costs really to alter. And the cycle starts up afresh.

7 *March*

Who can seize all that a look conveys ?
I listen to a brother. One word heavily
follows another. If there were only words,
I should be unable to understand completely. But in his eyes there shines a
fierce struggle — the refusal to serve himself at another's expense.

8 *March*

What can christians do to promote
development ? Above all, help make men
— and especially christians — more conscious of the injustice and inequalities
in the present distribution of wealth.
Generation after generation, in time and
out of time, reawaken the hardened conscience of our societies.

We know that what we do remains
symbolic. Only nations have sufficient
means to change the situation. If states

are at present shunning their responsibilities, we must make up for them temporarily.

9 March

Dryness in the personal encounter with Christ. Nothing seems to be happening. The days pass, time runs on. Even the value of the searching only appears later. It is certainly not to be more at ease in oneself that one perseveres in this fidelity. What is at stake lies elsewhere, and it is greater.

Common prayer too has its deserts to cross — but it is lived out with many others, we see faces and it overflows into a celebration of friendship.

16 March

Sunday morning in Paris with my mother, my sisters and their children who have come to visit us. A brother celebrated the eucharist. The day's reading was the multiplication of the loaves and fishes. Ever since my early childhood, I have experienced the reality of this text. My mother used to assure me that we would always have enough to fill us, and much, much more. As a tiny child, I used to long for there to be an organ in the parish church. To which she would reply, 'One day, you will have one'.

After the eucharist, I am reluctant to go to a mass. I should be sure to meet many friends there, I should want to invite them, and I only have very few days of holiday with my mother and sisters.

Now my sisters have gone out, to mass or to morning prayers. Everything breathes peace. Peace resting in the light that for a second floods the white page I am covering with the thick pencil strokes that compose my writing.

Hanging on the wall of my room is a catalan Christ, with the four evangelists at his right hand. His outstretched hand blesses us by night and by day. Green golds predominate. The artist can have had nothing but gold and pale green on his palette.

All the doors have been left open. In every room someone is writing. At the far end, my mother is installed. At 89 she still works every morning on her correspondance. In the room next to hers is the oldest of all my nieces. In the dining room a brother has set himself at the big table, also to write. I go to the gramophone to play over once more the 'Stabat Mater' by Pergolesi.

17 March

Went shopping in the big store in the Rue de Rennes. Going down to the toy counter, I ask what cheap items they have for children. Timidly the salesgirl tells me : 'Father, last Sunday I heard you speak on the midday news, talking about Latin America. And I told my husband, "I know him, Father comes to my counter".' She sells me eighteen dolls, reduced in price, and eagerly runs off to look for other toys in the stocks.

Not content with that, she asks her colleagues to look to see if they have other things that do not cost very much.

Opposite the toys is the jewelry counter. The salesgirl there, a coloured girl, tells me : 'You keep my counter for me for a minute, while I go and see my friend — she's bound to have something for you.'

23 March

When I returned to Taizé, I learned of the death of a portuguese immigrant at

Cormatin. He leaves eight children, some still only babies. This afternoon at their house the oldest son told me of his father's last hours. Struck down by a haemorrhage, he insists on seeing the priest to confess, be anointed and communicate. Then for the last three days he comforts his family and reassures everyone coming to see him that they will all meet again, with Christ. He keeps a picture of the Virgin of Fatima before him. He keeps kissing the picture and saying, 'The Virgin is here'. His last words are for her. Sometimes he weeps, but never when his wife is there.

This afternoon we told each other how this death can only bring us closer together. Before parting, we kneel. First, the mother makes her children kiss the picture of the Virgin, then she prays in Portuguese. The two smallest do not know how to make the sign of the cross and she asks them to repeat the Gloria, pronouncing it better.

Back home, I tell my brothers of the visit. I ask : 'In spite of the subsequent political uses made of it, why should not the Mother of Christ have appeared to three children of Fatima to comfort the poor of a people that was to suffer so much ? Little matter if the image described by the children is not to our taste. Any apparition is always impossible to translate into pictures.'

2 April

Talk with five seminarians. They manifest a collective anxiety. I attempt to fix their minds on the essence of the Church's life ; they listen attentively. They are longing for something, but what, exactly ? What will become of them ? Will they have a share in building up, or breaking down, Christ's body ?

Next, amongst others, is an old couple. Their mutual love is so genuine ; she, silent, has eyes that convey a friendship with God.

Here, at the same spot, not long ago I received a young widower. And today I learn that he has taken his life. Why did I not realise then that he would come to that ? When I saw him, he had just lost his wife, nothing could console him. . . . I tried to reassure, but all I could see were two wide eyes flooded with tears ; I insisted that he should not remain alone for the moment ; he had children to live for. I was ready to take any steps to help him — to welcome them here for a while.

8 April

Earlier this year, we began singing a short gregorian hymn in Latin at Sunday evening compline. Today the question was : 'But whatever for, when you are not obliged to use latin ?' My reply : 'Because we are free men. In singing that age-old hymn, we are being anti-conformist.'

9 April

Trials, palpably, are with us. In former periods they would have brought me down, for a moment, by their sheer dead weight. But this evening I found myself telling a brother 'I am a man rich beyond measure'. By what am I blessed ? By our monastic calling, by the love of my brothers.

10 April

In our old societies, there is enormous scope for cancelling each other out. Behaviour is dominated by the fear of dangers. Little spring-time sap in a civilisation that has reached its autumn. Less new bursts forward that endure. Our spontaneities rarely know a second morning.

11 April

Three cows have just arrived at the house — we had previously given them all to the cooperative farm. With them here, we shall have a direct presence of one quality of rural life — the cycle of the seasons. In late autumn the three cows will settle in the stable ; sly visits late at night, when everything in the stalls breathes calm and warmth of welcome.

13 April

Yet again, a youth asks what prayer can be for him. To begin with, I tell him, 'Do not look for a solution that fails to take your humanity into account. Personally, without my body I should have no idea of how to pray. I am no angel, and I have no complaint about that. At certain periods I sense that I pray more with my body than with my understanding. Such prayer is at ground level — one's knees bent, prostrate, looking at the place where the eucharist is celebrated, taking advantage of the silence and even of the sounds coming up from the village. The body is well and truly present to listen, grasp, love. It would be sheer folly to want to leave it out of account !'

20 April

Longing for spring to arrive : the cold weather persists but the brilliance of the garden gains by it ; for three weeks now gold has been singing in the daffodils, red in the tulips. The freshness of the air makes them last.

At this period of the year I am always transported in my innermost heart ; I

want to miss nothing of the labouring of
the plants and trees ; so I set my working
table close against the high window filled
with daylight from the north. Then I
carry my papers to the desk near the
window that gives fully southward. A
disturbance in the air : already the first
squeaks of the lightly shaken shutters
announce an approaching squall ; it
comes, great drops whipping the southern
panes. I return to the north. And there,
nothing but peace, serenity. A misty
curtain, the rain driven in successive
waves, is mounting the valley from the
south.

On the rare occasions that I have
chanced to be in town at this season, the
springtime struck me as less glorious —
but there was the same cheerful gladness.
Even in town, I watch for signs : a bud,
sheltered by a high facade, bursting open
before many others ; the morning light ;

the freshly lit clouds chasing by, high above the roofs.

21 April

Progressive or conservative, the two attitudes may well spring from one source and have a regression as their real motivation. For the progressive, a regression towards adolescence, the age when things burst apart, when all continuity is seen as a snare. For the conservative, regression towards a far distant past, lying before birth — only what belongs to that period can be sound.

22 April

Living close to the earth, I need the city. There, man's creation lies at every turning. The imagination is awake, to grasp the way in which the relationships of a mass of people are harmonized.

51

Living close to the earth, conscious of the limitations that result from this sometimes excessive love for the creation, I need — if I am to understand people — to listen to those who are poles apart from myself. All men, whether they know it or not, are penetrated by the waves of contemporary thinking. Rather than remain unaware, I want to understand and I am granted here on the hill moments when I listen to men pursuing research in various fields : theology, information, psycho-analysis, Marxism . . .

Living close to the earth yet friend of the great cities, unanimity grows painfully within me, when we are gathered in our church with my brothers and many others.

23 April

In the southern languages the word for Church means meeting or — even better — assembly : 'ecclesia', 'église', 'iglesia', 'chiesa'. In northern languages the Church is designated by the name of the Lord (Kyrios) : 'church', 'Kirche', 'kyrka', 'kerk'. So there too south and north complement one another.

7 May

The body can only move by obeying the feet — and they only go ahead one after another. Man, if he hurries too much, loses breath. All the excess work, all the letters waiting to be answered are nothing to be upset over. One step after another, one job at the end of another.

8 May

The burden resulting from so many giving up and fleeing the Church is practically overwhelming. How unfathomable is faithlessness. Its hurt harrows my life. At these points Christ awaits us, in agony for each man.

9 May

Imagination, when it works out plans for the future of those concerned, may prevent us from grasping at the right moment God's intention.

And at the same time imagination, as a creative force, drives man out of himself and permits him to seek some change, some transformation, for other people.

10 May

It is good to write each day and if necessary to oblige myself to do so. It is my handwork, as another man pounds dough and bakes bread. It is the means of a fundamental independance.

12 May

Heat invades the hill ; at dawn I went to spy the mist-bathed garden through the narrow bathroom window ; I lay down again ; on reawakening, summer had burst through.

When I was a child, I would make my song of this 12th May. From top to bottom of the house I used to thunder 'Today's my birthday, the best day of the year !' Out in the garden, I would go to see if a peony had opened during the night ; I used to encourage it by forcing apart the protective petals to set free the crown.

This morning, as in the past, I went to look at the peonies. They were still shut.

Returning from the morning's common prayer, brilliant sunshine was bathing the oak standing at the bend in the path between the church and the house

55

— we call it the 'oak of Mamre'; I was surrounded by brothers laughing to see my enthusiasm at living this day, when I am 54 years old.

A thought crosses my mind : today will go without a hitch. In the mail, nothing difficult ; among the greetings, a letter that I had confidently been expecting for a long while ; suddenly, a telephone call from outside. It goes on and on ; will he never finish ? A jolt for this day : I had so wished to live it peacefully.

This evening, another telephone call, from Chicago : warm, joyful voices ; my brothers . . .

20 May

The refusal of efficiency becomes an effective sign that corresponds fully to the needs of mankind.

56

24 May

At the present time I often go to the small village church, close to the reserved sacrament. There is a presence there — witnessed to by the faith of the Catholic Church since the first centuries.

Why do I never go before the reserve of eucharistic bread that we keep on a small altar after our Taizé eucharist ? Could it be that the faith of our parent Churches is not thus confirmed by the custom of centuries ?

30 May

Every man is branded for life by the encounters of his earliest years. When I was five, I spent one Sunday with my sisters in the region of Estavayer. Late in the afternoon, returning to the harbour from which we would cross the lake, we went into a catholic church. Everything was veiled in shadows. The light shining before the Virgin and the eucharistic reserve has remained an unimpaired image in me.

A few years later I went to Besançon with my parents to visit an uncle. Opposite the house lay a church. I shall never know why, but one morning, I rose before any of the others, and went into the church where mass was being celebrated. On my return I found the family breakfasting. They were all amazed that I had gone out so early and it was hard for me to say where I had been, because of my uncle, as though I had somehow compromised him.

6 June

To set one's own person forward leads invariably to hopelessness.

In my life as a man, marked by christians unable to understand our vocation at Taizé, it takes all my watchfulness not to look for compensations. Like blame, praise poisons. It stimulates for a moment, when one has been humiliated by seeing one's intentions distorted. But one hurt is scarcely soothed before we come to desire more praise. Courting criticism would be of no help — as though the harshness of judgements might cure us of the need to be reassured. Blame simply leaves man in doubt and confusion.

9 June

A few weeks ago, a german television service asked to interview me in my room. And the first question began 'You who are protestant . . .'

Spontaneously, an unexpected reply burst out : being protestant has meant, for over four centuries now, protesting against the Catholic Church. But I do not protest against her. If I sometimes express a refusal, it is just as much against certain protestant attitudes as against catholic ones.

What an idea to programme one's life on protest !

11 June

Before waking, a dream : someone invisible lays a figure of Christ in my hands. I speak a word of happiness, I forget just what . . . Christ very close to me : that's all, I am not interested in knowing anything more.

12 June

This morning a Jesuit asked me : when you say you wish to see the ecumenical vocation lived-out, rather than talked about, does that imply that you are opposed to research into doctrinal questions ? And my reply : several times each day, we pray the liturgy — the prayer of the Church of all ages — and gradually we absorb the great themes of the faith, theology soaks into us. You see, without that prayer, we would never have sung and lived the Resurrection to such an extent. The celebration of Christ comes first, but the need to express it in theological terms follows automatically, as a direct consequence.

Besides, theology is surely also situated in an intimacy between man and God ? If it is knowledge without contemplation, it loses all its creativity. What is harder than a man whose theological scholarship is not flooded by the freshness of a communion with an Other ?

13 June

For months past, one thing has been preoccupying me : with the present discord in the Church, what act could give peace to those who are shaken and strength to those who are committed ?

I sense that such an act should be a gathering of an exacting nature, regularly repeated for the years to come. Over a certain period of time, building and searching together. And with that, again and again the same thought dominates : this demanding gathering is going to be a council of youth. But who will carry it out ? As far as we are concerned, there is no comparison between the effort needed and our possibilities.

Besides, if we set out in that direction, what trials lie in store ! Oppositions are bound to arise, and peace and friendship are valuable beyond price. Where to draw new courage ?

24 June

With four of my brothers two days spent on a visit to the bishop of Crema in northern Italy. My room is high in the house. This morning, from my bed, my eyes could not tear themselves away from the lombardic frieze running around the cathedral. To think that I am here, in the home of one who so genuinely bears witness ! From my window, waiting for it to be time for mass, I could look down on the two sisters on a lower floor — coming and going with hushed steps, opening shutters, watering the flowers on the terrace, replacing a faded geranium by a fresh one. I had to wait for the bishop — always an early riser — to wake. He had stayed up too late because of us last night. At last, his shutters swung open.

Meanwhile, I strolled as far as a tiny door leading off the terrace. Behind it, buried in the thickness of the cathedral wall, lies a minute loggia opening into the church. The sanctuary was bathed in pale gold. In the presence of an early morning congregation, priests were celebrating mass according to the new texts. In their gestures, their movement — first to the lectern, then to the altar — I beheld an unexpected dance : David's joy before the Ark.

25 June

Today with the bishop, we pursued yesterday's conversations. I was anxious that he should realise one thing : all that I came to confide to him, to hear his opinion on, is likely to lead me, with my brothers, into new commitments. After so many years of struggle, I appreciate the quietness and calm of recent months. Shall I have the courage to adopt some daring new venture for Christ and his Church ? I realised this morning, as I awoke, that I was afraid. Where to find the courage ?

Two hours after our final conversation, the five of us were at Sotto-il-Monte, the home village of John XXIII. Arriving at the house belonging to the Roncallis, we see, standing by the gate of the yard, the old peasant Zaverio Roncalli. He is astonishingly like his brother, Pope John. I met him once before, but he seems not to remember. Talking with us, he pronounces a word : 'Corraggio' and adds, in his rugged dialect : 'Sempre avanti' (ever onwards).

We go to the parish church where his brother was baptised, and sing some psalms, an alleluia, and stay for a while in the silence of these haunts of a childhood. As we are about to leave we agree, with one accord, that we want to see once more the house of Zaverio Roncalli. He is still at the same spot. I remind him of his two words. He asks who is driving : 'He drives, you bless.' And then he adds, raising one finger, 'Sempre Spirito' (always the Spirit) — and these last words 'Mai paura' (never fear).

We had not come to ask him for anything. The man speaking these words is poor, and very old. He cannot know what he gives with a few syllables. The best that we have to live for others, we must perhaps ourselves ever remain unaware of.

Dialogue

PRAYER
AND POLITICAL COMMITMENT

Brother Roger, what does prayer mean to you ?

I am asked that more often than any other question. It is true that prayer lies at the very heart of our life.

Prayer is first of all waiting. It is allowing the 'Come, Lord !' of the Apocalypse to well up in oneself, day after day. Come for mankind ! Come for us all ! Come for me !

It is not the privilege of a few. It is a reality easily accessible, for tiny children as for old men. It finds expression in innumerable ways.

In the course of our days, and nights, there are gestures that we accomplish on account of Christ, and such gestures become prayer : forgiveness, reconciliation, some struggle to remain faithful — in marriage or in celibacy offered to God. These signs, and many others, are a language that we address to Christ. They are accomplished for his sake, and show him our love.

Insofar as prayer remains the expectation of Him who is not I, it is neither flight nor projection of myself. There comes the moment when I can only say : you are the other, you are he who exists as himself.

In the encounter with this Other, our intentions are purified, our heart finds limpidity. Before this Christ who exists in himself, who could keep up any pretence ?

How do contemplation and political commitment go together ?

Through contemplation, day after day we are able to stand back from things. At the level of any political commitment, it frees us from self-seeking. So it is something vital for any person wishing to undertake daring political actions. It enables him to refrain from seeking ways of imposing his own ideas, and not to desire unconsciously his own success, but only to serve.

In politics, there are men who are tempted to make use of Christ for their own personal ends. It is up to them to be lucid and to rid themselves of that. Contemplation permits us to become aware of all our thoughts and not to be ashamed of any, to order our values before the face of Christ and, as regards our own political involvement, to discover whether or not Christ has some place there.

Is the community of Taizé politically involved ?

So long as political involvement means committing all one's life for man and taking part in the building up of society, then such has been our intention from the very first day.

Here, at the beginning, in 1940, it meant taking political refugees into the house. Which in turn signified, at that period, withstanding the strongest pressures I have had to bear in my whole life, because I was still quite alone at Taizé.

Later, in 1952, as soon as we were twelve brothers, certain of us went from Taizé to live in industrial, working-class areas, at the very heart of the fight for justice. And, today as ever, reading the letters arriving from our various small fraternities, I can easily judge to what an extent several of my brothers are exposing their lives.

At Taizé itself, for certain of us, it has long meant different commitments in rural cooperatives and syndicates.

But I have always felt it necessary to distinguish between belonging to a political party and adopting a position in favour of justice. Our community, with the demand that we be a parable of unity, does not leave room for us to belong to other human families — some political party, for example. On the other hand, I would always want us to be dominated by a deep desire to give our life for mankind.

How is violence against others — inevitable in any revolution — to be reconciled with the demand to love all without exception ?

Man has received, first of all, an ability to convince : attempting to persuade those who oppress by using all the available means — words if possible, passive resistance. . . .

But when all the available means of persuasion have been exhausted, and in case of 'clear and prolonged tyranny which seriously offends the basic rights of the human person and dangerously harms the common good' (Paul VI, 'Populorum Progressio'), does not violence then become a necessary choice, as a way of setting men free ? It is not possible to reach this extreme without a mind purified of all self-seeking. And never forget : 'He who strikes with the sword will die by the sword.'

How could I ever be in favour of violence as such ? The Gospel within me contests any such idea. By it I learn of the presence of God in every man, hence the care for every human life. And yet, suddenly, I realize : I am in communication with certain young people who, as christians, have opted for revolutionary violence. When the oppressive violence of a whole society is such that it even claims lives, surely one must try to throttle that violence by an opposing form of violence ? I cannot answer this question for others, but I can maintain a communion with those who have come to such extreme positions.

Given the politicisation of so many young christians, will the Council of Youth follow in the same direction ?

From the start there was clearly indicated a political stand in favour of other men : 'Give our life so that man be no longer victim of man.' So it seems inconceivable that the Council of Youth should remain uncommitted in the realm of political life. Supposing that it did, we here at Taizé would not unduly force things, but we would certainly want to know the reasons. The Council would fail in its mission, if nothing were undertaken with a view to justice among men.

I remind myself that a man with tremendous spiritual authority committed multitudes of christians to an irreversible political option for more justice. And the consequences are incalculable. John XXIII, in 1962, called on all rural christians to embark on a process of 'socialisation' — something quite new. Later, in another encyclical, he called for a 'world government'. This second intuition is like a seed sown in the ground — and today the younger generations are tilling that ground with all their might.

Journal — extracts

JULY — DECEMBER 1969

2 July 1969

Burning heat, banished tonight by a strong wind. The windows and shutters have begun to rattle, it is one in the morning.

All around the house, a flood of cool air ; a perfumed wave soaks into my room, hitherto scorchingly hot, and brings peace. There was no hint of this sudden change coming. In the evening, towards the west, enormous white clouds fringed with gold were towering into the sky.

79

Sunsets fascinate me, whatever the season. Enraptured, I could stand watching for endless hours. My dream is to have a window giving onto a vast western horizon. Filled by all that the day had brought, I could remain alone before these signs of the infinite without ever noticing my solitude.

This year I often seek out, in the evening, the glow that to the north continues late in the distant darkness. And rising with the dawn I hasten into the garden, better to realise the shortness of the night.

Awaiting the day ! In the present convulsions of society, certain persons already sense the splendour of the coming day. Only things ardently awaited take on a great power for joy.

3 July

Worried this morning, having to find someone to write a text about Taizé. The time-limit has expired. If we do not choose for ourselves, the publishers will commission a writer — and perhaps he will be unable to understand us.

One name comes to mind : Jean Vivien. But how to contact him that rapidly ? Besides, a heart-attack brought him only recently to the very edge of the grave.

Then, this afternoon, I learn that Jean Vivien happens to be at Taizé, just passing through. I can scarcely believe it. I tell him what is bothering me. Without hesitation he agrees to write for us. We understand each other now as well as on the first day we met.

5 July

I have been to see O. on his hospital bed. Why does he have to undergo these repeated trials ? The burns on his face mask that look of limpidity that has ever

been for me an invitation to openness,
all through the seventeen years that he
has been a brother.

6 July

Yesterday at Mâcon, going to buy
some thermometers in a shop I had never
been into before, the vendor asked me if
it was for Taizé. But how could he know
where I come from ? In the car, I ask P.
about it. He assures me that it frequently
happens, in different stores in Mâcon. We
must all have a family likeness, built up
bit by bit. This is true for all those who
have to sustain a single struggle together
and who remain attentive one to another.

7 July

This morning a card arrived announc-
ing the death of Marie Braillard, at the
age of 84. I knew her when I was very
young. Only a few days ago, I was in

Switzerland with some of the brothers and we decided on the spur of the moment to make a detour by way of Chapelle-sur-Oron. There I enter the farm that belongs to the Braillard family — the last time I was there was at least fifteen years ago. I find Marie Braillard sitting talking in the kitchen. She recognises me directly : holding my hands she says, 'Roger, you are here — and I had been asking that I might see you again before I die. The other day the radio said that you were at Geneva for our Pope's visit and that made me so happy. My niece has always been too shy to write to you, but we often talk about you.' And five days after, she died.

14 July

Settled, fine weather has returned. The birds are quiet, overwhelmed by the heat. From a great height, two skylarks cry their clear song.

16 July

Yet another catholic exhorts me to free Taizé of all reference to the hierarchical Church — for him it is doomed, it means nothing to men : by our desire to maintain a communion with it, we are tying our own hands.

I have nothing to reply. Of course, I too wonder how authority will be exercised in the Church in the future. After being identified, in every Church, with juridical and temporal power ; after leaning for support on political power to such an extent : how is authority now going to right itself vigorously enough for it to be clear that its driving force comes from elsewhere ? With the passing of time, most — not to say all — of the reformation Churches have fallen into this same snare. But I also know that at present the hierarchy is purifying itself :

it could not simply disappear, or the whole body would promptly fall apart — of that I am convinced.

20 July

Twenty-five years ago today, the unsuccessful attempt on Hitler's life. In this particular case, destructive violence — the killing of a man — would have set millions free. We would have been spared those last ten months of war, when atrocities multiplied so appallingly in the concentration camps and in the occupied lands. And the massacre of the German resistance families would have been avoided.

Today two men will reach the moon. This research led by its first results to the destruction of whole cities ; since then, the same scientists have been preparing a new dawn, full of promises.

30 July

Rediscovery of the gentleness of certain late afternoons that announce the coming autumn. Fullness. Nothing more precious than the stone bench at the west corner of the garden belonging to my sister Geneviève. Time stands still.

I asked young monks from St. Benoît-sur-Loire this question : desacralising is at its height, yet we seem to be effecting a resacralisation without realising it — sacralising all that is instantaneous or provisional ? I may have contributed to this movement, partly by publishing 'Power of the Provisional' — so I am told, and I am prepared to believe it. But I regret nothing. In that book I tried, it is true, to express the present aspirations towards spontaneity — at a time when they could only just be sensed — but setting them in close complementarity with the essential continuities of a whole lifetime.

31 July

Tiredness, since rising. Could I have forgotten what are the sources of refreshment ? Entrusting cares and opponents to God sets free new energy — enables us to look beyond situations, and beyond persons. It is then, perhaps, that we touch a fragment of eternity ?

1 August

A young Venezuelan was saying at table today how, in the early periods of the Church, christians regarded heresy, first of all, as being lack of charity — and less as wandering away from orthodoxy of belief.

5 August

Night of the Transfiguration — festival of the present age. Our century has uncovered depths in man vast enough for him to sum up within himself the whole of humanity, from its origins until now. But to these vastnesses underlying the human person is offered a trans-figuration.

9 August

Letter from the aged aunt of a brother. She had heard a broadcast recorded at Taizé and from the Jura farm where she lives alone, writes, 'In this agitated world there is a secret movement — visible just here and there. Let us go forward.'

10 August

A new tendency is becoming clear among the thousands of young people who have stayed at Taizé this year. A few years ago, it would have been usual for them to challenge any man who, in their eyes, represented authority. The great wish was for the death of the Church's institutions. This year the search for Christ predominates.

Yet this morning I was constantly under attack — not by young lay-people but by religious and priests. The separator has kept back a choice zone of action for himself. He is hard at work at the heart of the Church, amongst the people who have consented for their whole life to exercise a ministry. Originally, many of them were of a will to purify the Church. That has now changed into hostility, or sometimes hatred.

I can only repeat : despising the Church, you are destroying yourselves — you are members of the body of Jesus Christ. But their choice seems to have been made.

11 August

Tonight we should have seen the largest number of shooting stars ; but the sky is overcast. We had forgotten what it was like, after four weeks of hot weather — the host of stars sheltering the hill beneath a vast, spangled cloak.

13 August

Surely in a sense the Catholic Church, all through its history, being the 'catholica', is constantly seeking ways — after the failures when it turns in on itself — of being a place of communion for the multitudes ? If present trials make it more fragile, they also cause it to become more permeable. I have confidence in it because, in spite of all the scleroses, it has offered the means of living by the promises of Christ : 'This is my body' and 'whatever you unbind on earth will be unbound in heaven'.

14 August

On my writing-table, a bunch of flowers — purple and orange, crowned by three sunflowers. A background of ivy leaves to carry the different strands of the polyphony. I cannot concentrate on the empty page ; irresistibly my eyes lift and my heart overflows.

One of the letters in this morning's post was from O. To read it fills me with happiness. I simply cannot believe it is meant for me : 'I have not ceased to remember you and our talk before I left. You are ever the brother I would want . . . all the things that unite us, these last seventeen years, fill my heart and help me discern God's will in spite of life's contradictions. With you I advance from my night towards the light of Christ.'

15 August

Last night's prayer, at three in the morning, was completely simple. At our midday meal, I threw out the question for my brothers of there being such a prayer every night — guaranteed by just a few. Then if someone finds himself awake in the night, he could have the delight of joining his brothers in the church.

It is almost seven ; this evening I am writing with my window open towards the blue line of the distant heights that drop down towards the Chalonnais. The fountain is uttering the same note as in the middle of last night.

16 August

The weight of all the struggling ! I consent to fight — there is beauty even in trials — but not to let vital forces be eaten away, without which I could no longer gather up all my energy in order to continue.

17 August

In the church we have begun to read the second Letter of Peter. My attitude in listening is rather that of someone who has just received a letter from one of Christ's contemporaries. Every word tells. Peter's faith — it counts, in life !

18 August

Talk with M. about what characterises our vocation. In recent years we have given much importance to making everybody welcome here. But supposing that this were to the detriment of some absolute bound up with our calling ? Is it clear enough that the call constantly to follow Christ marks in us a line of separation ?

19 August

This morning I glimpse Pablo Cano out on the road : 'Hello, Señor Pablo ! Vicente has left, you are on your own now.' 'Yes — all alone.' We say good morning — then I hear him calling me back : 'Brother Roger ! Not alone ; every day, our God is there' — laying his hand over his heart.

A long walk with G. At the end of our conversation he asks me, 'What is most vital for you in our vocation ?' At the moment, I see three main values : prayer, love for the Church, the search for justice.

20 August

Twenty-nine years ago today, I first discovered the village of Taizé. Within the community, I have always preferred the day to pass without being observed in any way.

From the very beginnings of Taizé, here in this cut-off spot man — with or without God — victim of the powerful, is present to me day after day.

22 August

Yesterday and today breakfast shared with young people. Their trust is touching. Do they realise the struggle that is being fought within themselves by certain of the brothers whom they admire ?

Over the years, our relationship with the young people who come onto the hill for a few days has changed. At first, we did not venture very far in our exchanges with them. But today we touch on what lies at the very centre of our life. As these quiet, simple exchanges unroll, every expression, every glance has its importance.

At the end of the midday prayer I stopped to say a few words to a brother in the sacristy. A man came up and told me his name, as though I knew him. He asked me if I would put my signature in two of my books — something I always find hard, but I did not dare to refuse this sign of friendship. Quietly in my ear, he whispered, 'I had given up the priesthood ; but I am going to be a priest again. The Church is suffering.' I do not

know if it was he or I who added, 'The
Church is suffering! And so we cannot
leave her.' And he withdrew after promising to write.

23 August

I learn that Aldrin, the Apollo XI
astronaut, took with him bread and wine
consecrated at the eucharist. Once on the
moon, he prayed and took communion.

24 August

This morning, visit from an unknown
bishop with fifteen priests, from Italy.
Returning from the church, we talk of
Christ's words 'This is my body' and I
ask, 'Will the catholic eucharist for ever
remain closed to non-catholics? Is there
no issue possible?' The bishop talks to
me of patience in latin. The expression
hurts I find, and I am surprised with my-

self when I insist : supposing this moment of history were not going to recur for a long while ? I can already sense that all expectation is vanishing amongst the young.

26 August

Could it be that christians are no longer bearers of good news ? Nowadays as I reach the religious news in the newspapers, I find nothing but sadness about the Church. And over the last two years or so, I can see the consequences. Men and women who once loved the Church with every fibre of their being have begun to be suspicious of it. Then other men and women think it necessary to counter that and start crusades. The sadness of the present times is diluting any vigour by which to push forward. What joyful news is there that could bear along the largest number of people ?

28 August

This evening our church is packed. Why do so many young people keep coming here ? The best thing they can give is to uphold our waiting. But how can we uphold theirs ? What can we do except listen, trying to understand what quickens them ?

4 September

This morning, during the common prayer, I suddenly become aware of the quality of my brothers and I am moved to the depths of my heart. They give their life — all their life. They pay dearly the price of their commitment. I know that better than any. Then I can no longer say if my admiration is for my brothers or for Christ who has so set his mark on them.

6 September

A boy asked to see me, to say that he could not understand our giving up the fraternities of young people. His face, normally full of joy, was drenched with tears. And it has stayed with me all day long.

I explained how, in a number of these fraternities where young people lived for one year or two in a house together, the weakest elements had dominated. Through generosity towards them the others — at the outset determined to live out the demands of the Gospel — finally relativised the call of Christ. Gradually the salt had been loosing its savour.

This evening, I continue to ask myself questions. I accept that I must take a large share of responsibility for the impasse we have reached with these young people. My idea had been : surely young men and women could share our experience for a time ? Is there not some way of trying to live during a limited period what we live for a whole lifetime ?

Today, little cells of the Church often spring up — fraternal, temporary. They cleave to what men live, hide there, become invisible. They belong to the underground movement of the Church. They are more or less everywhere. Like the cells of a body, they are born, subdivide, disappear. Some cease to exist for a time and then re-form afterwards.

Although there is this possibility of their rising up under a new form, I suffer from having had to put a stop to the youth-fraternities : was I really compassionate ? Whenever I am obliged to say 'no' in order to keep someone within the dynamic of what is provisional, I am always afraid afterwards that I may have been less than merciful. Fortunately, this morning I was able to invite this particular boy to eat with us and we laughed together : laughter opens us towards a full humanity.

8 September

A girl writes that, as a christian, a revolution could bring her, if needed, to point a machine-gun at her parents and kill them. So destruction is lodged within her. Whether or not she actually commits the action 'with a view to greater justice for men' as she says, the break within her is already complete.

9 September

A question written by one of the young people here : 'You talk of suffering in the heart of the Church. One can sense that what you are talking about is precise and alive for you : for me it is something vague and exterior ; but your sharing in this suffering makes me ask myself quest-

101

ions. What really is this hurt at the Church's heart ? And then : what part can young people have in a parable of the love of Christ in the Church and for the world ?'

11 September

My mother begins her ninetieth year. Leaving the church today, she was surrounded by friends and she said to one, who at once noted it down, 'I know that in what lies beyond I shall praise God constantly. And since praise is already the best part of my life here on this earth, what wonders of beauty I shall know then !'

12 September

Only reconciliation will bring a breath of freshness, of festivity to the Church.

Early this century, Pius X opened the catholic eucharist to tiny children and by so doing he provoked a new burst of life that no one had dared hope for. He freed christians from a conscience overburdened with scruples about communicating. And today, what bishop of Rome — leading activator of reconciliation — will have the interior strength to make a simple gesture : to open the catholic communion to all those who, not catholics, consider in the eucharist the reality of the presence of Christ ; and so provoke a burst of reconciliation ?

29 September

Some people think that living in the country means being cut off, away from the world. The world ! Man bears it along as he goes — even in his most total deserts. Personally I find nothing easier than living in the centre of a large city, where I can be alone. The world is neither more nor less present there than in the peace of the fields.

17 October

A young jesuit from Colombia wonders why the brothers are in general untouched by the theology of Bultmann 'yet you are not men to refuse to consider any contemporary line of thought ?'

What is at stake lies elsewhere and is so much more important : to make the Church and the earth places for men to live. It lies in a conscientising of every man : man becoming aware of himself, of his thoughts, of his worth, of the gifts of God set within him — since God is present in every man.

Our strength is limited, hence a choice is necessary. What we lose on one side we gain on the other — where we reckon that the fate of mankind is being played out. Is anyone capable of fighting on several fronts simultaneously ?

26 October

I am in the church, talking with a group of forty men, when suddenly I see one of them — quite young — collapse. Two of his friends carry him out of the group and lay him at the foot of the altar, where he begins to come to himself. His drawn face, covered in perspiration, shows that he is really not well. A doctor is sent for, and he orders tea to be brought. But the patient refuses, with the words 'No, not here'. He could not bear to drink anything at the spot where the eucharist is celebrated. There is something noble in that attitude. 'No, not here' : I find everything in those three words, they fill me. And yet I am not at all shocked when young people, if there are crowds here in cold weather, install their mattresses and spend the night in the church — even at this very spot at the foot of the altar.

27 October

Some students come to ask me how they can work out a common rule for the year they are going to spend as interns. A rule ! The term is so juridical ! Yet I also used the word, twenty years ago, when I composed the short text that indicates the bases for our life. I suggest that they ask themselves questions that begin with the context they are in. 'Like many young people, you refuse privileges ; yet your studies mean that you are certain to acquire them, and will perhaps lead you to positions of power. Are you going to prepare yourselves to dominate men, or to serve them ?'

28 October

This morning I was trying to think which single word best characterises my life. I found only one reply : fidelity.

In the village church, a number of

young people kneeling or prostrate, searching for a moment's stillness. And in burst some noisy women, anxious to visit everything. Someone points out that this is a place for prayer ; so out come rosaries, manipulated with gusto. And soon the chattering starts up again. You can say that they are contesting the silence.

A very old woman is also there sometimes. She too prays the rosary — but how devoutly !

30 October

Outside the window, summer is still there. Today the light bathes everything in a clear blue.

R. wants to talk about his work. How to teach computer-programming 10 kilometers away from Taizé and still maintain the priority of the common prayer ? I reassure him : in him there is no dichotomy between scientific studies and our common creation. Whatever he may feel, in fact he has managed to integrate the two. But he pays the price demanded by his searching.

7 November

Why so much love for the house ? The fire burning in the fireplace will warm my room all through the winter ; since this morning drops of rain have been running down my window panes, after months of drought. I have carried the desk to the window. I cannot complete one sentence without raising my eyes, so afraid I am of missing some change, the brightness edging the long clouds, the patches of clear sky. The Far East in the sky above Burgundy !

8 November

Prayer ? A whole universe. On certain

days I feel like dancing to express my praise. I talked about that with Mrs R. The first time I met her, with her motionless features, I took her to be a puritan of distinction. I was unaware that she was head of a school of dance in an American university. Then one day I saw her dance the 'Stabat Mater' by Pergolesi : she was a different person.

I asked her then about the use of dance in the Church. She reflected first and only gave me her reply some time later : 'We westerners cannot simply ignore our inhibitions. Dancing during worship is somehow artificial. But, adapted to our possibilities, quite imperceptible movements are enough to express it. In that way I can make even paralytics dance, by suggesting that they think of the movements and try to make them imperceptibly. Dance exists potentially within every person — the main thing is to live it with the imagination, if there is no other way possible.'

10 November

In me is a man who does not consider himself necessary. How is it that the confirmations that come from those I love simply spread over the surface, evaporating at the first blow ?

The wind is blowing from the east, squall upon squall since early morning. The constant noise is tiring. I begin to long for the town.

12 November

To Mâcon to buy Christmas gifts. Coming down the last hill, overlooking Mâcon, we have a view of the Jura as I have never seen it before, in all its depth.

Mâcon delights me as much today as on the day I first discovered it, one hot morning in August 1940. I have been

110

through many towns. But the landscape along the Saône ; the road winding from the old bridge up to the Place de la Barre ; the Place aux Herbes — friendly as none other at Christmas time ; all these attract me and always express the same sense of welcome.

Beside the Saône nasturtiums are still in flower — there cannot have been any frost here, whereas at Taizé the gardens have gone dead over the last ten days beneath the freezing nights.

The return to Taizé means driving through the Bois Clair, then dropping down into the blue valley beyond, across empty countryside. The houses that are inhabited smile at me.

As I was waking this morning, the night's last dream had me on a hill near Mâcon, at the top of a tower where, with my sister Geneviève and others, we were waiting for the sun to come up. First, from behind the Jura there appeared great fountains of light rising into the sky, then disappearing to be replaced by others in a magnificent display. Then the sun began to appear. And once more all was plunged into darkness. No one expressed surprise ; such was the rule of the game. Vivid sense of joy at the vision.

I remind myself that I was born in the Jura, with just such a vast panorama before my eyes.

15 November

Picked chrysanthemums and marigolds in the garden. The late autumn : richly tinted skies — shades of violet and orange. Already, in the shelter of the house, the jasmin is promising its first flowers.

22 November

This afternoon we arrived at Rome.

We had been so looking forward to coming down through Italy and viewing the autumn. We found nothing but fog and pouring rain. Everything lost under a dim twilight, when we had been expecting a glorious morning.

To the Corso for our first walk. At the opposite corner of the block in which we live is the church of Santa Maria in Via Lata. It was built over the house where St Paul is said to have lived while under arrest. It is now open again, after being closed for restorations for years past. Sisters are there to maintain a constant presence of prayer until late at night. Angelo Roncalli, the future John XXIII, lived in the flat attached to this church as a young priest. He used to pray at this spot. Festival springs up in my heart.

In the church are several youths, hesitating at the door a father with his small son ; we exchange a smile.

25 November

Today Pope John would have been 88 years old. I am reading the letters he wrote to his family. Poverty-stricken priest that he was, he loved his people, sustaining them as best he could.

The flat is full of peace. This evening we were saying that even if it is different, silence is present here as at Taizé. In the yard the water is spurting and bubbling in the fountain.

The moon pierces through the grey, brown clouds. At the centre of towns it shows itself as nowhere else, rising above the mists tinted with all the accumulated smoke. Poetry does not die in the big cities.

Man can create. If some of his discoveries lead to the pollution of water and air, he will find ways of making things good. Although I know that the constant increase in population calls for fantastic means of development, I am confident in man's capacity to create. Where technology is concerned, optimism prevails.

26 November

The bishop invited to this evening's meal is overflowing with benevolence. At table we laugh a great deal — in fact, so much that I find myself obliged to add certain funny details, to help one of my brothers with an uncontrollable fit of laughter. But everything is taken in good part. And in the exuberance of our conversation we touch on serious themes — themes I shall be touching on again during the many talks I have with all kinds of different partners in the days to come.

27 November

More and more convinced of one thing : our community will only be able to hold true if it can anticipate a communion with the Bishop of Rome — without at all denying our original spiritual families by that.

28 November

Faithful to our Roman habits, we went at about 11 pm to take the last letters to the central post office. With me went a young brother due to set off tomorrow morning for the North East of Brazil. He will have to rise at dawn and, because he did not want to wake me then, I had already given him the blessing and we had taken our leave when we decided to go out for our walk.

Only two minutes before we reached the house again, he told me something that he had been keeping to himself for months past : a mutual friend, a priest, has asked to be reduced to the laity.

In a few seconds I saw the whole story over again : discovery at the Council of a young priest from Latin America, open faced, a broad smile, deep eyes with an inkling of sadness. His bishop could not have been more generous and the son was full of regards for the father. Loving both of them, I tried to understand.

What is that priest going to become once out of the priesthood ? This event is so hard to bear that I find I have suddenly grown older. Once alone in my room, tears flow as I try to grasp the mystery of this man's life.

30 November

Sunday in Rome — a long walk on the Palatine, letters that give pleasure to write, the telephone call from Taizé, an excursion through the crowded streets — at places they are swarming with people — the meal begun with a meditation on the Gospel by a young Latin-American, a prayer at 11pm in Santa Maria in Via Lata : all things that go to make up a day filled with festival.

3 December

Certain present-day trends incline towards a pluralism without unanimity. In the Church the result is a body without a heart. And immediately a struggle ensues between those who are interested solely in the diversity of the different members and those who, by reaction, try to impose an outsized heart. In a monastic community, this would mean that more or less at once there would be no way of living a parable of unity.

5 December

A festive morning — with a rendezvous at the Secretariat of State. In the Vatican there is a strong family spirit — inevitable with the warm humanity of the Italians ! The two lift-men are both friends for me. At the end of the gallery a uniformed Swiss guard salutes. I ask

'Did we meet during the Council?' He replies 'No ; but I was with you at Geneva on the boat carrying the Pope.' There is an old bishop sitting there, tired and looking sad. We share a few words. Then I am accosted by two priests who know me, and one is the young bishop of S. in central Italy. After our meeting, I take the lift in the company of an Italian priest ; he tells me that he has been at Taizé several times. On the way out, yet more signs of friendship from those at the reception, all very simple but very human : the face of God in these faces, they are poor.

7 December

At moments, in the stillness of my Roman room, I realise how certain reforms in the Church may only affect the surface of things. It is not those who say 'Lord, Lord' who do the will of the Father.

And it is not those who say 'reform,
aggiornamento' who are the most recept-
ive. It is good to wash the outside of the
cup, but if it is not limpid within, then
what will become of us ?

9 December

Letter to a Latin-American priest :
'Step by step I am with you in the
terrible struggle you have undertaken for
those whom others — including us christians — have left aside. Living with the
poorest of men, your service goes beyond
what is humanly possible . . .

I recall your inner combat. And my
thought is : true, reforms are essential
for the people of God — but only on one
condition, that men themselves be trans-
formed.

I meet old men who have difficulty in
seeing the need for the renewals. But they
are full of goodness and with them the

gifts of the heart, pastoral concern, make up for many failings. Such men do not hinder those who entrust themselves to them.

But at the moment many in the Church applaud the various reforms ; younger, much younger than the others, they think that by consenting with their intellect they are fully within the aggiornamento. And yet, certain of these middle-aged men, lacking any human or pastoral understanding, will not let themselves be interrogated by the present failures. Far from encouraging, their attitude holds back and imprisons the most generous christians.

Now I am in that period of life and you are about to enter it. How can we defend ourselves against this lack of understanding, against hardness towards any man — and particularly towards those who cause harm to others ?'

17 December

Today, private audience with Paul VI. Full of joy, the Pope's welcoming words were so generous towards Taizé that I dare not repeat them. Then our exchange opens, and goes far. The Pope intends to celebrate mass for Taizé on December 31st.

29 December

Returned to Taizé ten days ago with broncho-pneumonia. Illness and work together had robbed me of all my strength. The two brothers who are doctors stressed that I was to remain in bed, even for the Christmas midnight mass. But that evening one of them was himself confined to bed with flu, and the other was on duty at the hospital at Mâcon. So I was free to go against instructions. And here I am up, ready to carry on.

Each day I stay in the church, talking there with young people. One question was 'What does sin mean?' It is not an easy thing to talk about today. The psychological sciences have taught us how in every person there lies a pre-determined pattern of disorder. Children have suffered at the hands of their parents, but those parents were themselves traumatised in their early upbringing. The individual finds himself relieved of a whole burden of responsibilities resulting from the succession of his forefathers. And what then is sin? It is there whenever I deliberately prefer my own will to that of Christ, whenever instead of serving man I make him my slave.

31 December

The last hours of the year, and I am filled with a flood of joy. I live in such thankfulness that the trials of the moment are light to bear.

The sight of countless young faces — the people from different countries here at Taizé — persuades me that with them we shall be able to build something for mankind and for the Church.

To live through the trials of the Church and to love her still more because of them.

Gratitude for H. and G. our first two catholic brothers. Gratitude for each of my brothers without exception.

I believe that I find the ultimate joy in accepting that one day I shall leave life on earth for a life that will have no end. I do not worry how God's eternity will be, I have better things to do than conjure up images of paradise. But the knowledge that I shall be able to close my eyes in peace and encounter Christ is a source of festival. Consenting to our own death opens towards a flood of life.

Dialogue

A FESTIVAL,
BEGINNING AT DAWN

Who are you ?

I am Roger, your brother. I love my name because I received it from my seven sisters. When I was born, to celebrate the event my parents called them together and they chose the name I bear.

How can you live for so long in community without somehow falling into a routine ? What is the source of renewal ?

As concerns the inner life, no one is privileged. Whoever we be, we are always obliged to begin anew each day, rediscovering each morning both the crosses and the festival within.

What allows us to persevere is a commitment made for our whole life — a yes that is not open to revision. Some days it can become heavy, and no longer springs spontaneously ; for a period then, the commitment undertaken before God is observed as a law. It is the same for those who live the conjugal faithfulness of marriage. From time to time, we need the law as a tutor. But not for too long ! There always comes the moment when festival returns.

Now that there are Catholic brothers at Taizé, has anything changed in your life ?

The unity of different peoples is achieved by inter-marriage — so mingling races. And for christians too, after many centuries of separation : being together in our diversity will be one way of attaining visible unity.

The presence of Catholic brothers amongst us has obliged us to be concrete, to refuse answers that remain theoretical. These men have strong points of reference. At the heart of their life is a unanimity of belief. So they present us with the question of the Church.

Living with them, where do we differ ? Nowhere except that by their life they pose us the question of the ministry of a universal pastor. Why someone to provoke unity at the heart of the Church ? Why the service of a shepherd for the largest number of christians ?

The presence of our Catholic brothers saves us from those useless ecumenical exchanges that do not end in unity. It forces us to ask : what is unity ? Can the visible unity of all christians be restored without a visible centre, without a universal pastor ?

True, the ministry of the servant of the servants of God is burdened with an enormous weight of history. The layer upon layer of clothing added during the ages make it hard for his unique service to shine through. But if we do not believe in such a ministry, who is going to speak in our name to all men in times of crisis ? Who will make present a living word of Christ, valid for the whole people of God, at a given moment ?

Our festival risks being a brief flare-up : How can it be a fire that keeps on burning ?

For several years now, I return constantly to a thought of Saint Athanasius, discovered by one of my young brothers :

'The risen Christ makes of man's life a continual festival.' When the brother first uttered those words to me, I did not say anything, but thought : that 'continual' is almost too much.

Today, I think that Saint Athanasius knew why he said what he did. Our existence as christians means living continuously the paschal mystery : a succession of little deaths, followed by the beginnings of a resurrection. That is the origin of our festival. From there every way lies open ; our life can go forward, making use of what is good and of what is less than good. Festival re-surfaces even at moments when we scarcely know what is happening to us, even in our hardest trial : a break in a deep relationship. The heart is broken but not hardened : it begins to live anew.

For you personally, brother Roger, how do you make life festive ?

First, by consenting to the humanity that is mine. Because of Christ, I know that nothing is lost. He gathers up everything to such an extent that, at each morning's waking, festival can dominate. Whatever the difficult event that may occur during the day, this intimate festival is an inner quickening, it modifies and transforms events, raises up the overwhelmed.

Festival is not the result of an artificial 'high'. Festival is built up. In life's monotony, little by little, a hidden brightness becomes manifest.

Meals are a way of renewing our festival. Do you know how I sometimes travel with my brothers ? Going by train we take our food with us. If it is evening we turn out the lights, then we light a big candle and invite the strangers there to eat with us ; so we enjoy a festival that is not just between ourselves but with those around us too.

The older I grow, the more I find my festival in the witnesses on whom I lean. Often, I read a few words of John XXIII. I loved him and it was mutual. I need his face, and I trust his prayer, since he is in God's eternity.

For festival, faces count even more than words. They express friendship, and friendship is the face of Christ. Nothing has more beauty than a face that a whole life of struggle and combat has rendered transparent. There are only beautiful faces, be they sad or radiant. My life is discerning in others what is ravaging them, what rejoices them ; it lies in communicating with the suffering and the joy of men.

FESTIVAL

Ever since I was a youth, my desire has been never to condemn. For me the essential, in the presence of some other person, has always been to understand him fully. When I manage to understand somebody, that is already a festival.

Journal — extracts

JANUARY — MAY 1970

1 January 1970

This year of 1970 will be one in which we shall dare to undertake new things.

Today's dialogue with the young people was a real battle. The ones asking the questions drove me back to my most basic positions. I was laughing inwardly, but sometimes it took my breath away.

We talked of the role of Mary today. She, a woman, is going to allow us to make a discovery. The Church has left it to men to take all the initiatives. Mary teaches us that initiatives are the concern

of women as well. She is the foremost
witness of the Church and summons man
to rid himself of his self-sufficiency, his
authoritarianism, in order to collaborate
with God.

The last question was about our con-
tacts with the working classes. My reply :
in our far-off fraternities there are new
possibilities. But in the region here, the
gates of the nearby factories were closed
to us when, living in fraternity thirty
kilometers from Taizé, we were reckoned
to be too clear about the real conditions
of the workers there. Since then it has
been impossible to find a job in any local
factory. Yet every day there are brothers
who go off to work near here.

What I ought to have added is that,
with the new year beginning, I cannot
see who is offering any real possibility of
greater justice. I have no confidence in
liberal democracies led by oligarchies,

and none in systems dominated by police repression, as in certain socialist countries. How to provoke a leap forward towards a just society ?

2 January

M. is back. He relates his mother's last day. Without saying anything to her family, she announces to someone there that she will die during the day. All continues normally. Those present pray Compline with her, as happens every evening. She prays more fervently for many of those entrusted to her. Then she says goodnight to her husband, and collapses : death had come.

Two days later her husband — an unpretentious man — sees her beside him. She is resplendent with light and insists, 'Do not be sad. Go quietly through these days. Know that now I am no longer of earth but of heaven.'

5 January

In the presence of others, a young Italian couple asks me to pronounce a few special words for them. He is a worker, his wife is fully occupied in a trade union movement. The question frightens me a little — I would prefer to avoid it. Their expressions are so open and appealing that I venture to ask them : you are attached to Christ, but how to serve him within his body, the Church ? That means not living somewhere between earth and heaven, but with both feet firmly planted on the ground.

6 January

Talked with Italians and Spaniards, all of them involved in the working world. As yesterday, the same concern about the Church. Of course, loving the Church for its own sake would lead to a disaster. For

140

'reasons of State', what injustices have men not committed in the course of history? Similarly, 'for reasons of Church', what has not been done? Loving the Church in isolation, without Christ, would end in intransigence. But loving Christ alone, without his body, encourages a narrowness within us. 'Loving Christ, loving the Church : the two are one' : words that challenge me ceaselessly.

7 January

Have set on the mantlepiece in my room a calendar brought back from Italy. Each day's date is very big, printed in red. So I can remember the day to be lived, today January 7 and no other : this day given for friendship, peace and joy. True a bad letter has arrived, but it has not been able to extinguish the latent fire.

141

8 January

Yesterday evening, conversation with a young poet. Hearing him, everything around took on new life and, in this cold winter, I could sense beneath the trees young shoots stir under the dead leaves.

10 January

The race to succeed, to get ahead at all costs : what devastation this is for christians ! When someone has no other means of regaining confidence in himself, he is doomed to dislocation, he empties away the best of himself.

11 January

Listen, always listen. Jo, an African economist, speaks of this in a new way. Listening, he says, is in Africa the function of the chief. Surrounded by others who help him to understand properly, he listens to each in turn. Then a direction becomes clear. Appearances notwithstanding, the head of a tribe often has a highly demanding life to live, since he is forced to listen to all.

12 January

These last weeks, A. comes home every day with new burdens scarcely bearable. For sixteen years now, so much energy spent sharing in the transformation of the living conditions of the least well-to-do peasants ! In the evening, I listen to him for a moment. What can I do except share his present anxiety ?

14 January

My sister Yvonne, just back from the Congo, had this story to tell about her four year-old grand-daughter Stephanie : she discovered that in the house next door a little African boy of the same age had to spend the whole day with the servants, without his parents. He cried constantly. So every evening, at nightfall, she would go to the bottom of the garden where a small hole in the wall gave onto the grounds next door. The little boy would be waiting for her and, through the hole, they held hands, having no common language to speak.

15 January

For the past two days a bishop from Brazil has been here. Once more I am given an insight into the treasury of faith, of sensitivity, into the creative capacity of the christians from that continent.

The relationship between us has been falsified by centuries of ecclesiastical exportation into Latin America. But today, in Latin America, men and women are arising who will come to evangelise all that in us remains impregnated with self-sufficiency, paganism, unbelief.

16 January

Letter to a young Italian catholic : 'To live Christ for men. To take part concretely, by giving all one's life, in the reawakening of a vocation proper to the catholic Church — as leaven of brotherly and visible unity within the whole community of men : surely that is our call and, henceforth, our common path.'

19 January

The beginning of the week of prayer for christian unity. Denominational immobility is more than ever apparent.

Yesterday many people from the region were gathered in our church. The priests were sitting among my brothers. The diocesan bishop preached. We live equally close every year. Yet we still remain apart for the eucharist, and we all believe in it with a common belief.

But optimism still does not desert me. The impossible opens the way to the possible.

20 January

This day, January 20, recalls to mind my father. Twenty-four years ago he was struck down with an illness that was to take his life within a few days.

A grey day — the weather could hardly be gloomier, but the lower reaches of the sky remain bright.

I strive to live as a man who knows his inevitable share of solitude.

23 January

Marked by conversations with someone so tense that all I could do was listen attentively and very receptively. At such moments I sometimes wonder : are these situations part of God's plan ? This morning the reply would have been : the Church carries all our humanity and a person's inner tensions are part of it.

27 January

Brief stay at Paris. Evening spent with a young astro-physicist from Bombay. I share with him this question which never leaves me : now that I sense Easter drawing near, I wonder if we shall have the strength to go ahead in a commitment with the young people. I should like to give up the idea of a council of youth.

When he left, I continued the same reflection : as far as I am concerned, nothing is serious, not even my own death. But in all this, it is not I who am concerned. Should I put a stop to what we have begun ? Would giving up be an act of betrayal towards the young ? Have I looked closely enough to see if the essential materials are available ?

28 January

Reading certain writings, even in very serious reviews I find so many invitations to lose touch ! The ideas are there. Then, with a little imagination, a tissue of gild- ed alibis is woven — more than enough to take leave of reality.

29 January

If I am with a non-believer, is the presence of Christ excluded ? His pres- ence is other, more I cannot grasp.

30 January

A youth asks me 'How do you see the service of authority in today's Church ?

How do you conceive of it for yourself, as Prior of Taizé ?'

Authority has too often been identified with a temporal power — but in the Church it is first of all a communion. Authority is neither monarchical, nor democratic : it is pastoral.

Personally I see my ministry as a service of unity. To be Prior of Taizé is, in my eyes, to be a man of communion.

Christ says of the shepherd that he gives his life, that he exposes it before the ravishing wolf ever ready to divide. I need a shred of the courage of Christ not to give up in the face of difficulty, not to flee, but on the contrary to promote unity, sometimes to arbitrate in situations, and to keep those who are mine in communion with the whole Church.

To carry out this ministry, power is of no interest to me. I simply know that our community has as its vocation to

live, each day, a parable of unity and that
it cannot do so without a servant, the
prior, who sums up the whole.

Such a service of unity does not set
the one exercising it at the top of a
pyramid, but right in the midst of all.

1 February

All through the day, wherever I am
and whoever I may be talking to, I find
ways of watching what is happening in
the sky. The sight of creativity constantly
in action, so many shades of gold set off
by brilliant greys — joyfulness wells up
inside me ; it is not so hard to bear the
burden of contradictions.

2 February

Days when the manifold pressures on
me are so contradictory that I find myself
wondering : am I blind ? Is my own view

of things an illusion ? A deep underlying stillness makes it possible for me to withstand the assaults day by day.

3 February

The southern window admits a first trace of spring : far off, a fringe of changing light bordering the hills of Cluny. I would not want to miss a moment of this promise of delight.

4 February

Man is bearer of Christ, but that does not mean that Christ can be reduced to a 'man-centred dimension'. Then he would turn into a simple projection of ourselves.

5 February

A brother hands me a paper on which he has noted the conclusions of an inner debate. The most demanding part of what he lives for Christ brings him closer to his brothers. Perhaps it is the awareness of his poverty that gives him such transparency.

6 February

Talk with a young Italian. He has often been here without our having met. At Christmas, when I was talking with hundreds of young people, I noticed him. Why ? I could not say. From our first words, his clarity made me sure that he would be the young European to participate in the intercontinental team, to announce at Easter the news that is building up.

9 February

A man, about thirty, his eyes bright, interrupted me yesterday during the dialogue in the Church, to ask how to react to unfaithfulness towards Christ. Was my reply disappointing ? I said : Lent is coming. It is a time set apart for the examination of the inner man — forty days of celebration, when the joy of forgiveness is rediscovered.

This morning I saw the same man. He is a priest, and I understand what is at stake in his struggle. I could find nothing more telling than this to affirm : his yes, pronounced one day before Christ and the Church, involved, as for anyone, certain psychological motivations. Perhaps those around did not look enough to see if there was in him the minimum necessary to live within the priesthood. But a vocation cannot be reduced to simply psychological elements. His yes cannot be a total mistake, it remains the yes of faith.

At the same dialogue a youth, sitting fairly far back, asked me timidly :

'Brother, who, for you, is Christ ?' I have
never been asked that in public before.
I ask him his name. He is called Alain,
comes from the local mining region. I
suggest that he repeat the question in the
microphone. He expresses himself anew,
in a strong local accent.

For me, Christ is he by whom I live,
but also he after whom I, with you, am
searching.

16 February

For several days now, I have known
that at Easter we shall have television
cameras to retransmit on Eurovision, live,
the moment when the Council of Youth
is announced. The time is fixed necessarily in the late morning. I have only to
think of it to lose all joy. The young
people will be mainly coming to celebrate
the Resurrection. That is the essential.

154

We cannot risk troubling the liturgy of Easter morning by pressures due to the technical demands of a live broadcast two hours later. Today we agreed to telephone the producer, to ask him to put the broadcast off until Easter afternoon. He cannot. In that case, we shall give up the Eurovision, it will be for another time. Once the decision was made, it was as though the field lay open : free to be spontaneous !

17 February

There are christians who want to impose their concept of society by violence. Others strive hard for a stifling doctrinal rigidity. And others, at present, band together against pornography. Would Christ call us to organise ourselves in order to impose our views ?

Those crusading against eroticism, for example : what motives are they obeying ? Do they intend to protect others by a simple exterior morality that is incapable of changing what lies within men ? But purity of heart is not satisfied with apparent wholesomeness. It delves deeper, to rid men of hypocritical or calculating attitudes. And suppose that some were motivated by frustration ? The working out of a morality on the basis of unsatisfied desires has nothing to do with the Gospel.

23 February

Eight days spent travelling through Spain. Days overflowing with happiness. The liveliness of the Spanish people, especially in the South, provokes new vigour.

At Malaga in the evening we join the crowds filling the main streets. We struggle our way through the mass of humanity. The wide paving-stones, smooth as a skating rink, incite us to slide rather than walk. Out of all the confused uproar pierce the shrill notes of an andalusian song.

We go into a church. Youths are playing rhythms on the guitar to accompany unknown tunes. An old layman reads the Old Testament, a girl wearing a long, dark red coat goes to read the Epistle. Where am I ? In the deep south of Spain and, even in the Church, nothing is as it was. I have never been at a mass using rhythmic music and here I am, at the far edge of Europe, gripped by its expressive force.

24 February

We have reached one of the goals of our journey. Leaving the main road at Bassa, we set out down a narrow but still passable road and finally go thirty kilometers along a rough track. The further we go, the stronger become the wild golden tints of the earth. Three times we descend to the bottom of vast hollows scooped out of the plateau by centuries of erosion.

Campo Camara : high-perched village near the Sierra Sagra. Walking through the streets we hasten to the home of Pedro Cano. The entrance — door and window combined — stands half-open. I push it further and see him, huddled on a low chair against the hearth. He is there in the gloom, even more gaunt than a few years ago. He stretches out his arms to us ; his eyes afire, he grasps our hands in his own. Not just the family but all the neighbours as well are squeezed into the one narrow room with its beaten-earth floor. He insists on our taking something to eat. Only the head of the family and we, his three guests, are entitled to the bacon, wine and beer.

The shadows of the night come on. We must leave. Once back on the tarred road, I perceive that all three of us are silent. What could we have to say to one another ? We have seen a face of Christ.

M. has fallen asleep — and normally he can always find tales to fill the car with our laughing. P. accelerates ; nothing but the hum of the engine. To speed through the night coincides with a dream of my childhood.

12 March

Four days at Constantinople. Afterwards, what raises my hopes is the awareness that an 86 year-old man, the patriarch Athenagoras — with so few means at his disposal and in a complex political situation — can have an enormous impact both close at hand and far away.

I have heard words that I cannot repeat. They burn and have great weight.

He, servant of the unity of orthodoxy, has the greatness of the truly generous.

Until my last hour, I shall see him as he was when we left. He held his hands high as though presenting the eucharistic chalice and once more repeated : 'The cup and the breaking of the bread : there is no other solution : remember . . .'

14 March

My heart bleeds. Philippe's death, on February 25, has at last caught up with me. At first I had simply seen the event in the context of the communion of saints but after three weeks the humanity within me strikes back.

Philippe : brother of the beginnings. With him everything always ended in laughter. Ever since the news reached me in Spain, I have been wondering : what is the sense of this unexpected heart attack in a man so young ? Why this tearing apart ? Like so many others, confronted with a separation, I accept my lack of any reply.

23 March

Young people are here from every continent. Together we shall announce something new. I repeat to myself : beyond the event, God is waiting for us. Once we have launched into it, we shall hold firm. Among the young people is Maximinio, a young peasant from North East Brazil. Poor among the poor, when he arrived at Lisbon he had no jacket or overcoat. He wonders how our stomachs can take three meals a day.

28 March

Holy Saturday. I asked Maximinio to sit in my place, on my stool in the middle of the brothers, for the midday prayer.

An unusual gesture, not understood by all.

29 March — Easter

The 'joyful news' is announced, the Council of Youth will be the instrument by which to put it into effect.

Last night, I woke up with this thought : you will never manage it, the words will refuse to come out.

This afternoon, as I took the microphone to announce the Council of Youth, a young Italian whispered 'Brother Roger, speak up ; you must proclaim the announcement of the Council of Youth.' How well he knows me !

1 April

Peace of heart, in the centre of an enthusiastic crowd these last three days ! And peace of heart too when criticisms start surging up !

162

Monday evening, Maximinio left for home. He is a witness I lean on. I remain full of the blessing he gave as he set off : 'Receive my blessing ; blessed be the heart that is poor, reconciled and unified by Jesus Christ.' Before leaving me, he also said : 'Meu coração está cheio de felicidade.'

Our eyes have contemplated the faces of man victim of man : we have heard appeals rising from the depths of the abyss : Maximinio, Ann, Michael, Maria, Edna.

After the announcement of the Council of Youth, I had expected all kinds of misunderstandings to arise. I was wrong.

In my youth, fear sometimes prevailed. I could not see the reason for so many hopeless struggles. Again from 1948 to 1960, that same fear returned, this time because of the battle for the unity of the

Church. Today, having reached my present age, to keep the joy that ever remains !

8 April

'It is not those who see God who are saints, it is those who believe in Him' : St. Teresa of Avila.

14 April

At Geneva, during our visit to the World Council of Churches, there were moments of intensity — our prayer, the two meals. But the exchanges always remain less than what we would wish to communicate to one another. One can sense there a strong secularisation.

16 April

These days, when I put out my light before falling asleep, I am struck by a thought : perhaps this is the last time you will fall asleep on earth, the last time eyes will close which have been filled with the joy of earth's colours and harmonies.

18 April

We are witnessing a vast process of mutation in the human consciousness.

When asked to consider the men or things of the past, even the recent past, young people often employ a critical approach — a contestation. And this worldwide phenomenon is true of the youth of all societies, christians or not. Because, like all men, they suffer from a doubt about themselves, and to be reassured they affirm themselves brutally.

The enormous present-day increase in population has made youth discover its strength. And from there, some feel that they could have a share in the exercise of power or even simply take command by violence, with a view to creating the more just society to which they aspire.

Then too, it is by contestation that youth judges the real worth of its elders. They want to find out if they can really give their trust.

If we let this new attitude shake us or revolt us, we may no longer have any way of tackling basic themes together, and then dialogue breaks down.

19 April

All day I have been full of what I was thinking about yesterday. Who would have said, five years ago, that today I should have so many conversations with contestatory christians ? I remember the first shocks experienced at Taizé, during a huge gathering of young people. It was in 1966, long before the events of May '68.

A brother has just reminded me that in that same year, 1966, I wrote at the be-

ginning of 'Unanimity in Pluralism' :
'To desire pluralism for its own sake,
without a unanimity in what is fundamental, is to accept — sooner or later —
the death of faith on the earth. Scattered
apart, men are given over to mutual contestation.' I cannot recall writing those
words.

With the distance that age is gradually giving me, I come to distinguish two
distinct expressions of contestation
among young christians :

There is a small number for whom
contestation has become an end in itself.
If dialogue succeeds, there is a risk of
unleashing irrational and uncontrollable
impulses within them.

But then there is the vast majority :
those who allow the Gospel to contest
within them. They live by the Word that
touches them. How to be attentive to
them ? I often wonder : could Peter the

apostle also have been referring to them when he said : 'Listen to the prophetic word !'

Such young christians are fascinated by all that concerns prayer and faith, but they are afraid of being taken over by some system. They find it hard to understand why others distrust them, and set up so many protective barriers. Whatever the quality of the thinking lying behind the warnings, they have just the opposite effect to that intended. How to achieve the complimentarity needed between charismas and institutions, spontaneity and continuity ?

21 April

Beneath a leaden sky, spring is here. I no longer see it, I hear it.

Whilst I am talking with the former bishop of Autun, Mgr. Lebrun, a brother brings me a paper. Good news : the Pope, speaking from his window to the crowd on Sunday at midday, spoke about the difficulties of ecumenism, then about the orthodox Church. After insisting that there were positive signs, Paul VI spoke these words : 'We look towards Taizé with affectionate respect.'

28 April

Admiration, astonishment : these Gospel values open onto 'enthusiasm' — literally 'being seized by God'.

29 April

Yesterday I received Father V. Our accord has never been greater. I remind him how in 1949 we were awaiting the postulancy of the little brothers of Jesus at Taizé. But the catholic hierarchy refused to allow it. At that time, I was conscious that their coming could lead to our living a common undertaking. I felt : why create a new community when the little brothers of Charles de Foucauld come so close ? Unable to welcome them, we were obliged to mature without them the ecumenical vocation that has brought us to our present position. But I view them with the same admiration today as on the first day.

We talk of the preparation of the Council of Youth. Father V. proposes a fraternity on another continent, four or five brothers, living in common with us. To think we have had to wait twenty years !

Together, we went to the village church, where the eucharist is kept. Can I write this ? I have no wish for wonders that are beyond me : light — inner and outer — filled the place where we were. I did not linger, but rose, so greatly do I fear putting God to the test.

6 May

Yesterday evening, the birth of a child who is dear to me from the first : Jean-Christophe Rémy, a great-nephew, my sixty-seventh. Christophe — bearer of Christ : and I know he will be.

7 May

A man of some forty years asks me seriously how to find a second breath so as to hold firm in his vocation. For me, only one way : return time after time to the first beginnings — that moment when the decision to give all one's life scattered thick clouds and made happiness burst out. Welcoming afresh the initial discoveries into one's life remains a festive source that allows, not just a second breath, but a whole series of new breaths, until death.

10 May

Yesterday I was thinking : the Easter season is almost over. It has gone like lightning. And today I receive this note from a youth : 'Common prayer is a life ; it is not undergone, but lived. It is a celebration, not a discipline ... The silence is there, palpable, so true as to be almost sacramental. Beyond a personal piety where I only encounter the God of Good Friday, I have rediscovered the Christ of Easter.'

11 May

Faithful to my old habit of listening to the same pieces of music for several consecutive days, as I write I am playing a record of Bach's D-minor oboe concerto. In it I hear every human supplication, and a reply. I hear in colours. This music

172

is tinged with orange, as has been the year that ends for me today.

At this moment — 5.30 pm. — I can see, through my northern window, a clear sky filling with enormous white cumulus clouds. High up the wind is blowing, yet the willows close by are motionless. The wind drives the clouds one against another, then scatters them again. And I am here, my head raised, swallowed up in happiness.

12 May

On this birthday, I am overwhelmed by the kindness of my brothers and my family. This morning, a letter from R. This brother is ill again. During his long journey across Latin America his eyes have seen the face of trampled humanity. But, in his far-off solitude, he has also understood the dynamism of the younger generation. And at this very moment, I receive a birthday telegramme, sent by him from Buenos Aires : 'May your festival have no end . . .'